What makes it snow?

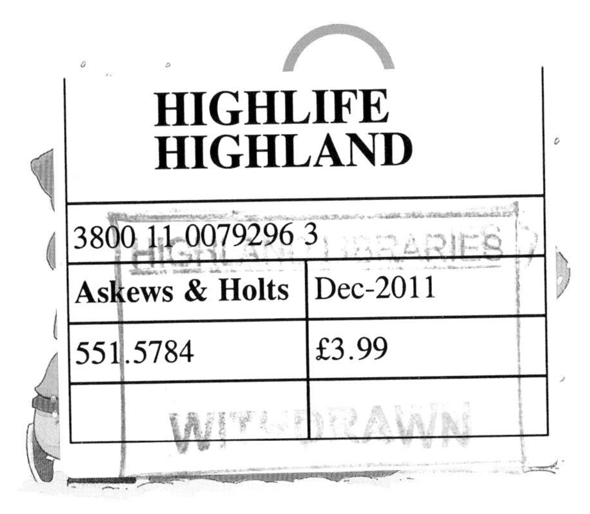

Paul Humphrey and Helena Ramsay

Illustrated by Stuart Trotter

First published in this edition in 2011 by
Evans Publishing Group
2A Portman Mansions
Chiltern Street
London W1U 6NR

www.evansbooks.co.uk

British Library Cataloguing in Publication Data
A CIP catalogue record for this book is available from the British Library

ISBN: 9780237544973

Planned and produced by Discovery Books
Cover designed by Rebecca Fox

For permission to reproduce copyright material the author and publishers gratefully acknowledge the following:: Bruce Coleman: (John Shaw) 10, (R Carr) 15, (Hans Rheinhard) 17, (Gordon Langsbury) 19, (Kim Taylor) 20, (Hans Rheinhard) 29; istock: cover; Robert Harding: 22; NHPA: 21; Oxford Scientific Films: 12

Printed by Great Wall Printing Company in Chai Wan, Hong Kong,
August 2011, Job Number 1672.

CONTENTS

Look, it's snowing! Let's go outside.
Hurray, we can make a snowman!

Let's get our toboggan out!

You must wear your warmest clothes. When the weather is as cold as this your bodies need a bit of help to keep warm.

I'm putting on my hat and my gloves as well as my coat.
I'm going to wear thick socks, too. I hate having cold toes.

It's still snowing. Let's try to catch the flakes!

It snows when the drops of water up in the clouds get very cold. Then they freeze and turn into ice. All the tiny ice crystals join together to make snowflakes.

Did you know that all snowflakes have six sides?

No, millions of snowflakes have fallen from the sky and nobody has ever found two exactly the same. But they do all have beautiful shapes and patterns.

You need to look through a magnifying glass to see them properly. Some of them are shaped liked stars and some like flowers.

Those are frost patterns. Frost is made out of ice crystals, too.

The air is full of tiny drops of water. When it is very cold outside the water drops freeze...

The flowerbeds are covered in snow.
I can't see our plants. Will they be all right?

Don't worry about them. The snow works like a blanket. It will keep all the plants underneath it warm by stopping heat escaping from the ground.

Yes, the leaves won't start to appear until it gets warmer.

That is because the snow muffles the sound, like talking into a pillow.

Yes, there are rabbit tracks, cat tracks and even tiny little bird tracks.

The birds are hungry. They can't dig for worms when the ground is covered in snow. Shall we feed them?

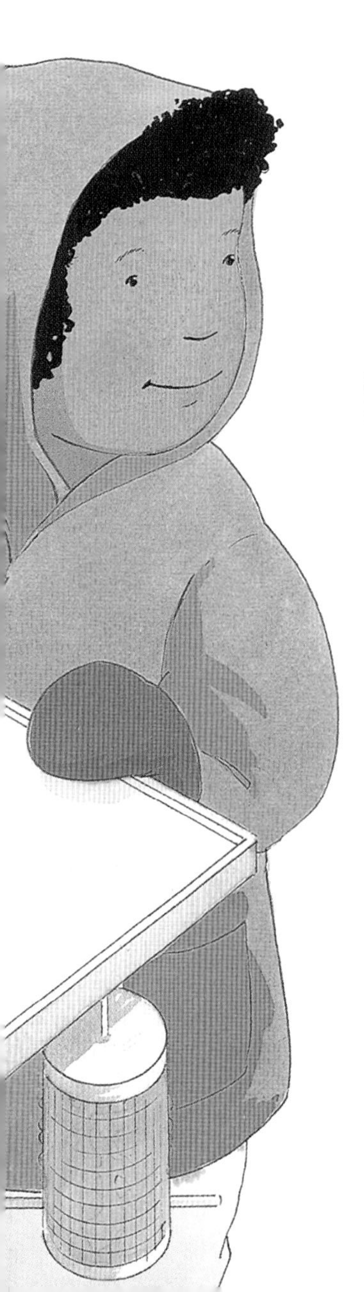

That's because it's so cold. They ruffle up their feathers to trap warm air and help to keep themselves warm.

Most of the smaller ones will stay in their holes and burrows to keep warm until the snow melts. The bigger ones will be all right because they have such warm, thick coats.

Did you know that some animals, like the Arctic hare, grow white coats in the winter so that they can't be seen?

There are some huge icicles over there.

When it's very cold, dripping water freezes to make icicles. Then, as more water runs down and freezes, the icicle gets longer.

Let's ride the toboggan.

Hold on tight. The toboggan will slide very quickly over the snow. When we get to the bottom of the hill we can go and look at the pond.

Look, the pond has frozen over.
What will happen to the fish?

The fish will be all right. They will be down at the bottom of the pond where there is no ice and the water is warmest. They can live like that for months if they need to.

When the weather gets warmer the snow will melt.

Yes he will, but melted snow is a very important source of water for the world. It soaks into the ground better than ordinary rainwater and it fills the rivers and the reservoirs.

I'm getting cold.
Let's go back indoors now.

Fun activities

Who's been here? See if you can match the footprints to the correct animal.

It's time for a snowy workout! Imagine you are somewhere really cold and snowy. How does the cold make you feel? In a group, act out being cold. Are you shivering? How can you warm your hands and feet up? Pretend you are a snowman or an icicle hanging from a building. What happens when it starts to heat up? Can you slowly melt to the ground?

Wrap up warm and get ready for a chilly adventure. Imagine you are riding on a toboggan through the snow. You could travel in an imaginary land or somewhere that you are familiar with, like your local park. Write a snow poem or story about your journey. What do you see along the way? Maybe there is frost or icicles. Do you spot any animals? How does it feel to be on the toboggan?

Interesting websites:

Make your very own snow shaker:
http://www.fingertipstv.com/ourmakes.php?makeid=149&step=1

Join these children as they explore snow in their garden:
http://www.bbc.co.uk/learningzone/clips/10639.flv

See if you can crack these snowflake puzzles:
http://www.metoffice.gov.uk/education/kids/fun_and_games_snowflake.html

Answers:
1. Cat 2. Mouse 3. Rabbit 4. Human 5. Bird 6. Deer

INDEX